TV MA

THE WHITE HOUSE

RCA

Editorial Cartoons by Kids 1998

Madison, Wisconsin

Published by:
Zino Press Children's Books
P.O. Box 52
Madison, Wisconsin 53701

Editorial Cartoons *by Kids* — 1998

All contributors to *Editorial Cartoons by Kids — 1998* have pledged that their work is original. Zino Press has, to the best of its ability, determined that cartoon ideas and drawings in this book are original to the cartoonists. Zino Press does not accept responsibility for the authenticity of any cartoons.

Zino Press Children's Books is a division of Knowledge Unlimited®, Inc.

ISBN 1-55933-213-1
ISSN-1093-2453

also available from Zino Press —

Editorial Cartoons by Kids — 1989
Editorial Cartoons by Kids — 1990
Editorial Cartoons by Kids — 1991
Editorial Cartoons by Kids — 1992
Editorial Cartoons by Kids — 1993
Editorial Cartoons by Kids — 1994
Editorial Cartoons by Kids — 1995
Editorial Cartoons by Kids — 1996
Editorial Cartoons by Kids — 1997

Foreword

by Mike Luckovich

Many adults think kids pay attention only to stuff like *South Park*. They'll realize how wrong they are after looking at this book full of editorial cartoons by kids!

These kids are not only aware of what's going on in this country and the world, they also have the intelligence to comment on issues in a cogent and often funny way.

Congratulations to all of you who made it into this book. Stay tuned into what's going on in the world. One day your generation will be in charge.

I have to go watch *South Park* now.

Mike Luckovich won the Pulitzer Prize for his political cartoons in 1995. His work appears in the *Atlanta Journal-Constitution*. Mr. Luckovich selected the prize winners in this year's NewsCurrents Student Editorial Cartoon Contest.

Introduction

by Dave Schreiner, Editor-in-Chief, *NewsCurrents*

Drawing an editorial cartoon is easier than thinking one up — and drawing one isn't easy. A good artist can add immeasurably to a great idea, but no cartoonist can save a bad idea. An editorial cartoonist has to distill a complex and often abstract idea into a single drawing. The cartoonist must know the issues and grasp the visual language of symbols, caricature, expression, and exaggeration. After all that, the cartoonist must draw something that addresses a single point. It doesn't matter if a reader laughs or gets angry at the cartoon. The cartoonist's real job is to provoke thought and debate.

For the tenth year, *NewsCurrents* and Zino Press welcome you to EDITORIAL CARTOONS BY KIDS. The 100 cartoons here are among the best of the more than 10,000 that came in to us during the 1998 *NewsCurrents* Student Editorial Cartoon Contest. We get these cartoons from elementary, middle, and high school students from across the nation. If you want to find out what issues interest students, take a look at this book. You'll learn about school funding, President Clinton's troubles, Saddam Hussein, and cloning. Topics range from immigration to whaling to Winnie-the-Pooh.

NewsCurrents is a current events program used by more than a million students weekly during the school year. We don't teach cartooning, but *NewsCurrents* encourages discussion and debate in the classroom and gives everyone in class a chance to take part. The *NewsCurrents* program tries to be educational, interesting, stimulating, thought-provoking, and fun. Just like editorial cartoons.

Writing and drawing editorial cartoons is especially demanding for students learning the fundamentals of a complex world. But after 10 years, we've come to expect incisive, provocative opinions about the state of the world. It may be the fresh perspective students bring to issues that delight us most. Their cartoons make us *think*.

Perhaps the toughest task the editors of NewsCurrents have each year is judging the 10,000 entries. There are well over 100 of them that could be published. But this year, we had some help. The prize winners were picked by Mike Luckovich, the Pulitzer Prize-winning editorial cartoonist for the *Atlanta Journal-Constitution*. We thank Mr. Luckovich for his help — and we thank the thousands of students who entered the contest and the marvelous teachers who inspired them. We applaud those students whose work appears here. We know you will, too.

Katie Seither

Grade 3

New Albany Elementary School

Cinnaminson, New Jersey

First Place Winner Elementary Level

1998 NewsCurrents Student Editorial Cartoon Contest

School Funding Cuts

Alexander Harnden

Grade 6
Oakwood School
North Hollywood, California

Second Place Winner Elementary Level
1998 NewsCurrents Student Editorial Cartoon Contest

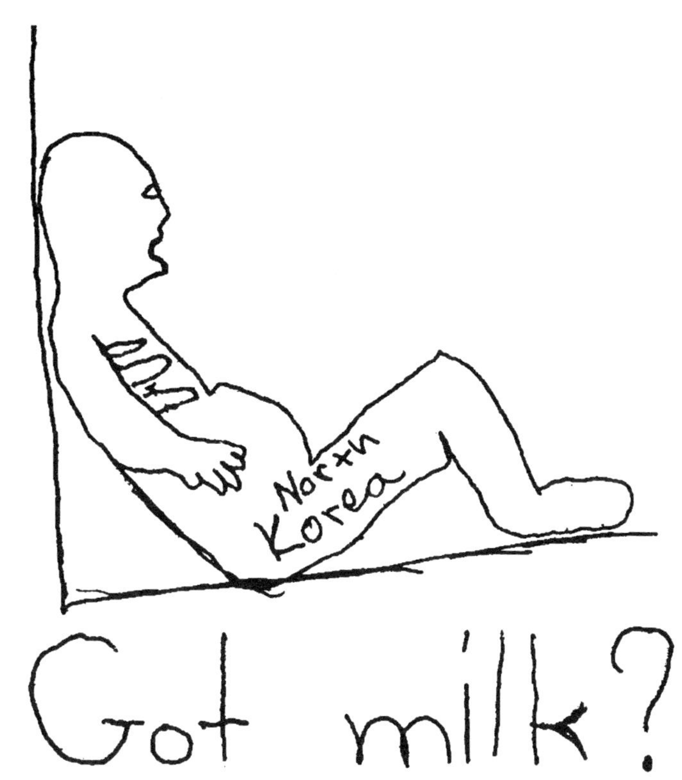
North Korea
Got milk?

Elizabeth Osterwisch

Grade 6

Carver Center

Gifted Education Midland (Midland ISD)

Midland, Texas

Second Place Winner Elementary Level

1998 NewsCurrents Student Editorial Cartoon Contest

Saddam Hussein
I love my people!
They make a great Shield!
SHPE
SHPE
US Army
US Army
US Army
US Army

Alexander Baron

Grade 6

Shadowbriar School

Houston, Texas

Third Place Winner Elementary Level

1998 NewsCurrents Student Editorial Cartoon Contest

USA SPACE SHUTTLE

There is one less Social Security bill we have to pay this month.

CLINTON

Hurry up, pops!

J. GLENN

Taylor Brown

Grade 6
Fort Mill Middle School
Fort Mill, South Carolina

Third Place Winner Elementary Level
1998 NewsCurrents Student Editorial Cartoon Contest

Got Ecoli?

Russell Olschner

Grade 6

Eisenhower Elementary School

New Orleans, Louisiana

Third Place Winner Elementary Level

1998 NewsCurrents Student Editorial Cartoon Contest

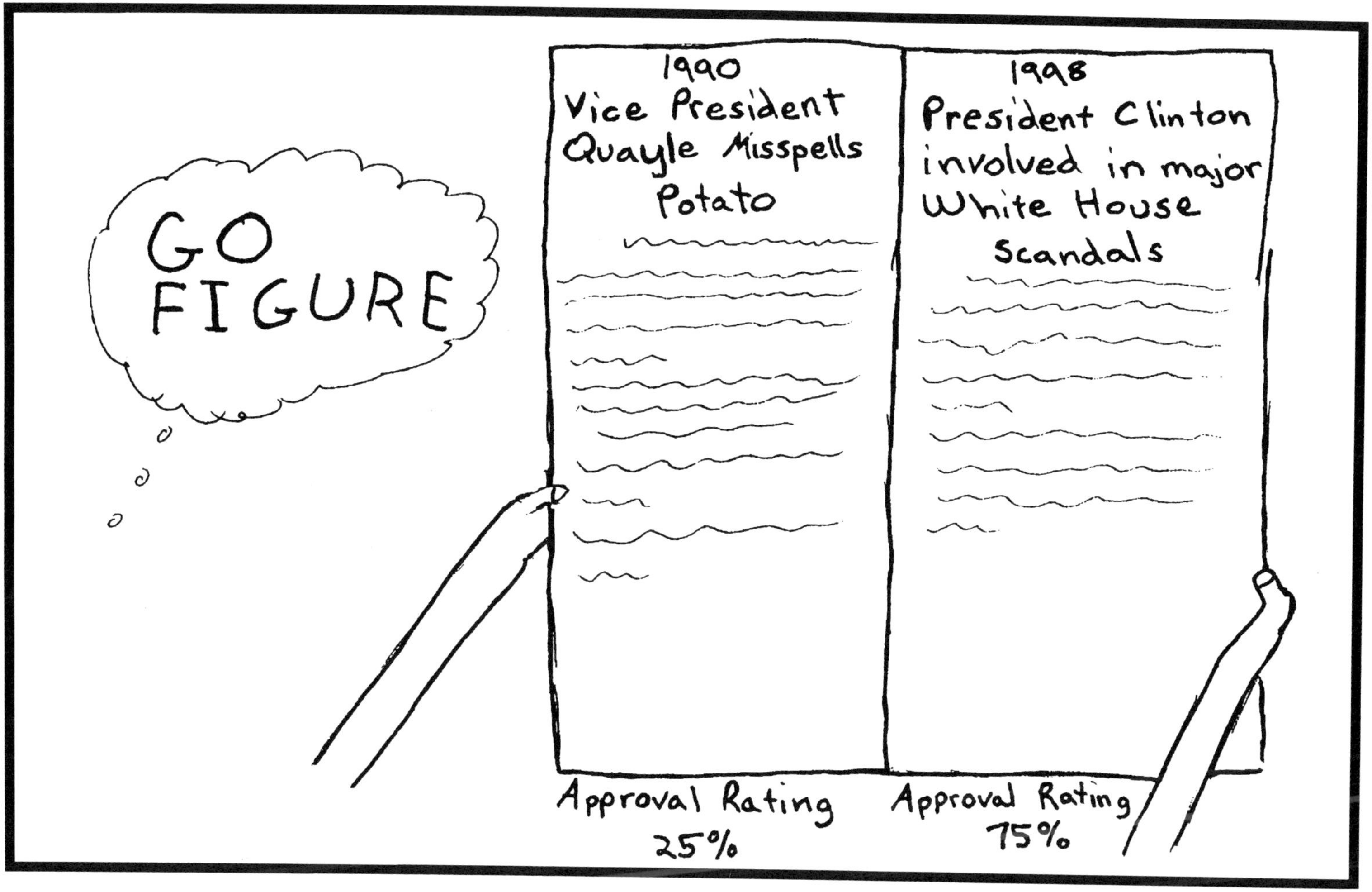

GO
FIGURE

1990
Vice President
Quayle Misspells
Potato

1998
President Clinton
involved in major
White House
Scandals

Approval Rating
25%

Approval Rating
75%

Eda Kuluslu

Grade 3
Del Prado Elementary School
Boca Raton, Florida

I wonder why Oprah came to my owner's beef company and branded me with this strange mark!!

Christopher Nowak

Grade 3
Monarch Bay Elementary School
Laguna Niguel, California

Through These rose colored glasses I don't notice crime AIDS, pollution, The Threat of nuclear war, political lies or cafeteria lunches.

CHRIS NOWAK

Janie Beaird

Grade 4
The Hockaday School
Dallas, Texas

"Boy! Next year I am definitely getting my flu shot!"

Nathan Rausch

Grade 4
New Albany Elementary School
Cinnaminson, New Jersey

NASA
SPEND $$ ON EARTH NOT MARS
We Need JOBS!
$$$ FOR HEALTHCARE NOT SPACE

Jay Bui

Grade 5

Columbia Elementary School

Annandale, Virginia

Oh no! I'ts burnt!
PEOPLE
EARTH
POllUTION & CO2

Natasha Doran

Grade 5
Jefferson Elementary School
Burbank, California

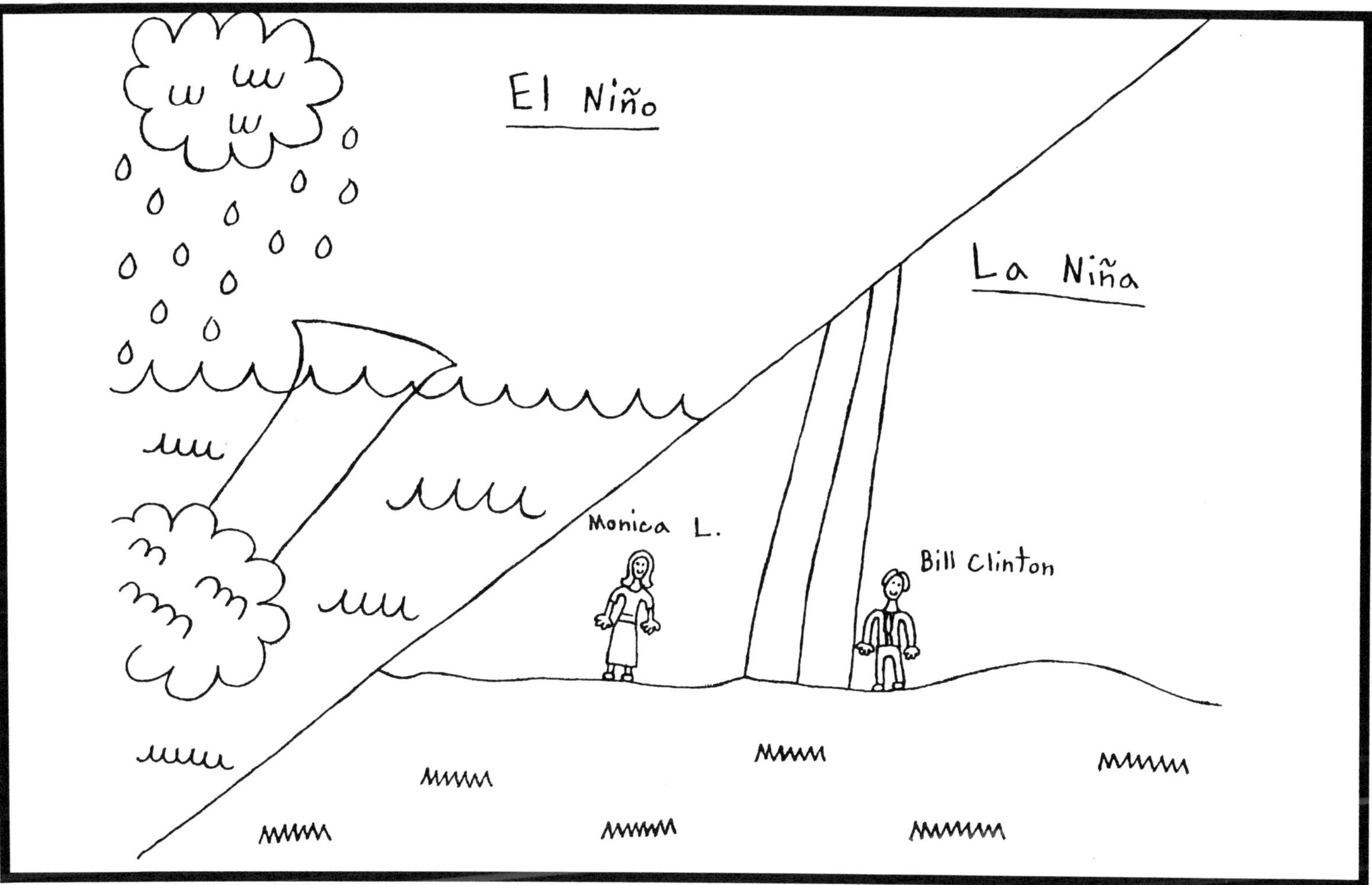
El Niño
La Niña
Monica L.
Bill Clinton

Natasha Nazar

Grade 5
Howard Drive Elementary School
Miami, Florida

Mr.Castro, it's not an imperialist Boomerang

Anna-Claire Rooney

Grade 5
St. James School
Basking Ridge, New Jersey

...and on my next vacation I'm going to Mars!
Tommy!! My Daddy says if you keep telling lies you'll be President some day.

Jeff Schaninger

Grade 5
Northside School
Fairport, New York

We will follow you, follow you wherever you may go. There isn't an ocean too deep or mountian too high it could keep, keep us away!
PAPARAZZI TRIO
Jeff Schanzer

Bevin Blaber

Grade 6
Albany Academy for Girls
Albany, New York

President Clinton
....and in school, every twelve year old should learn to log onto the Internet.
He can log onto the Internet, he just can't read!
AOL

Bevin Blaber

Grade 6
Albany Academy for Girls
Albany, New York

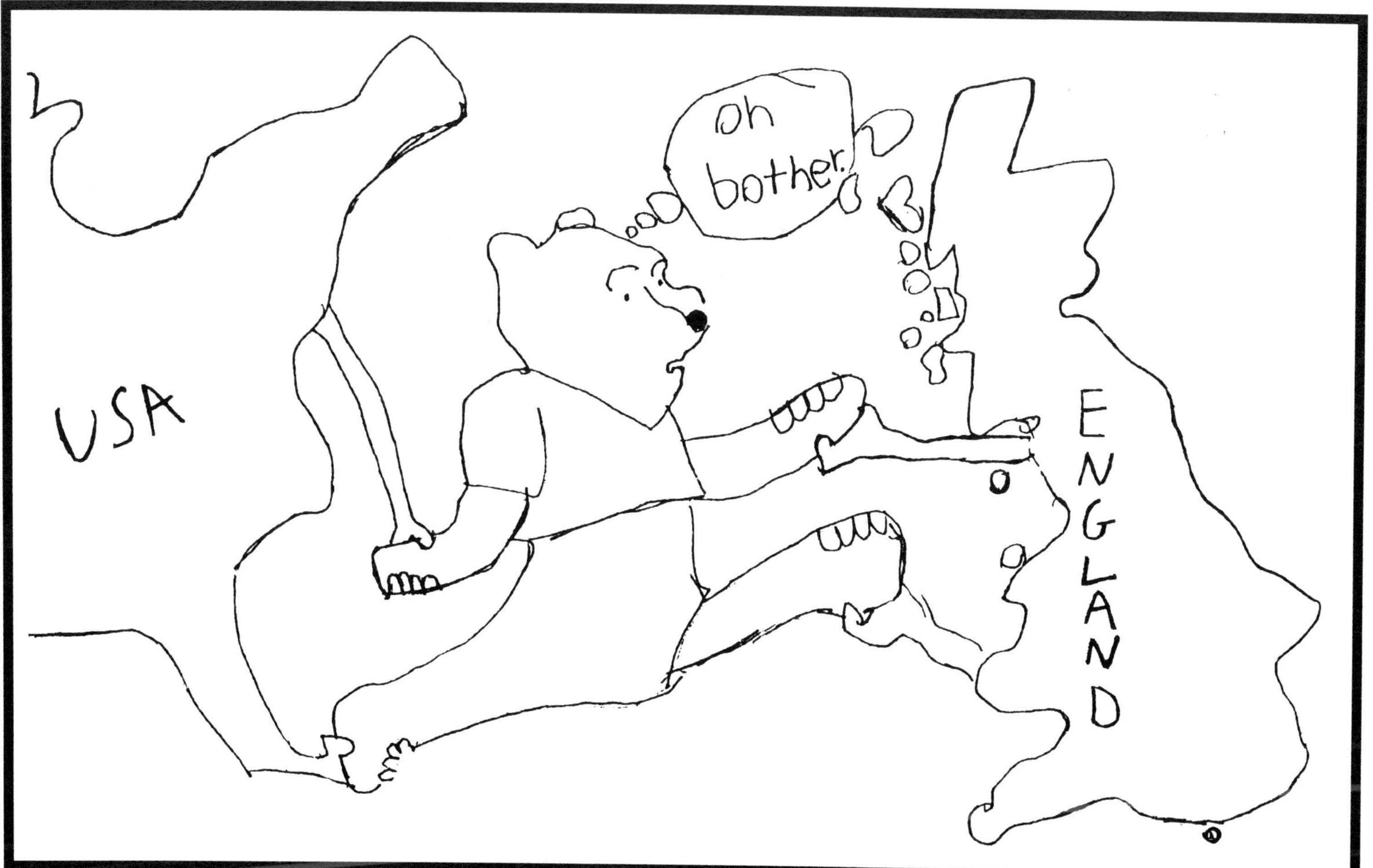
Oh bother.
USA
ENGLAND

Gina Cervino

Grade 6
Holy Family School
Orange, California

Burp
Where did all the whales go?

Zach Churan

Grade 6
Royal Oaks Elementary School
Sun Prairie, Wisconsin

Nagano 98

Nagano98

WHEATIES

McDonald's

NIKE

Going for the gold isn't just about medals anymore

Caroline Feinberg

Grade 6
Albany Academy for Girls
Albany, New York

United States

But not YOU, amigos!

Mexico (our neighbors)

Statue of Liberty

Give me your tired your poor, and huddled masses. I lift my lamp beside the golden door.

Restricting the U.S. to whom?

Caroline Feinberg

Grade 6
Albany Academy for Girls
Albany, New York

WHAT'S the Difference?

Michael (Drew) Frazier

Grade 6
Dupont Elementary School
Dupont, Indiana

Hey, Dad. can I use the line-item Veto ?
Chores
Feed Cat
Vacuum
Clean Toilets
Homework
Clean Room
E.C.

Randi Gebhart

Grade 6
Ironwood Elementary School
Phoenix, Arizona

1998
Let's go for a walk.
ANTHRAX MISSLE
UN
Agree ment form
Trash

Kate Golkow

Grade 6
Greenbriar West Elementary School
Fairfax, Virginia

Hey, do I look heroin chic now?
DIRECTOR

Nils Gould

Grade 6
Oakwood School
North Hollywood, California

Jessica Hryniewicki

Grade 6
Holy Family School
Orange, California

You boys need a few pointers?
Nagano '98
USA
USA
USA
USA

Matthew Layton

Grade 6
St. John's School
Binghamton, New York

Cloning

It was him.
It was him.
It was him.
It was him.
It was him.
Crime Lab

Social Security Office
Line Forms Here
It's mine.
It's mine.
It's mine.
Where Does It All End!?

Roger Mariscal

Grade 6
Field Middle School
Farmers Branch, Texas

on the internet no one knows you're a dog

Donna Moon

Grade 6
Shadowbriar School
Houston, Texas

Saddam
But That Would Be Wrong!

Ethan Schiff

Grade 6
Bolles School
Jacksonville, Florida

Teachers are very important to our kids
President
$3,000,000 a year
Jordan
23
$30,000 a year

Jessi Stewart

Grade 6

James Whitcomb Riley Elementary School

New Castle, Indiana

The Laboratory

oops!

What Idiots!

NO, you Idiot! I said CLONE

Cute hat

Ben Stickney

Grade 6
St. George School
St. George, Maine

Come (pant) back here (pant) NOW!
UN
Saddam
Nyah nyah!!
Biological Weapons

Jenny Streif

Grade 6
Westlake Elementary School
Indianapolis, Indiana

"... But the most wonderful thing about Tiggers is I'm the only one!"

Shannon Tate

Grade 6
Carver Center
Gifted Education Midland (Midland ISD)
Midland, Texas

Mir, Mir
on the wall,
How much
longer
'til we fall?
Shannon Tate '98

Arash Tehrani

Grade 6
Shadowbriar School
Houston, Texas

<Bill Clinton> Saddam we know you are hiding weapons. For instance is that a....
NO, It Is a Chair. That's a coffee table. That is a Lamp
acid
weapons
Bombs

Danielle Haselby

Grade 7
Marshfield Junior High School
Marshfield, Wisconsin

First Place Winner Intermediate Level
1998 NewsCurrents Student Editorial Cartoon Contest

Kenneth Starr working on the investigation

Erik Keselica

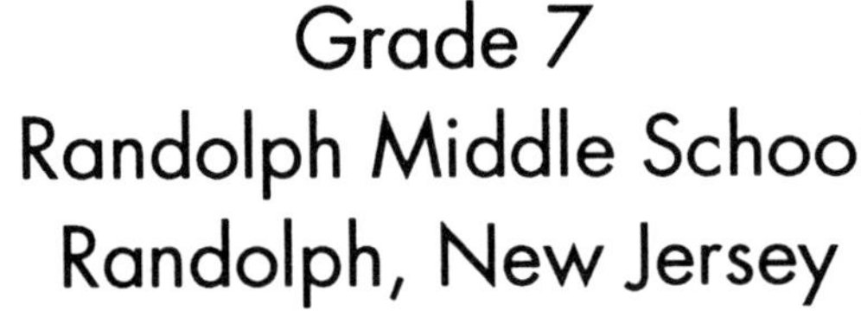

Grade 7
Randolph Middle School
Randolph, New Jersey

Second Place Winner Intermediate Level
1998 NewsCurrents Student Editorial Cartoon Contest

"Saddam Hussein becomes desperate in ways to hide weapons."
He
He
He
Grampa
USA
USA

Jesse Swanson

Grade 7

Reeths-Puffer Middle School

Muskegon, Michigan

Second Place Winner Intermediate Level

1998 NewsCurrents Student Editorial Cartoon Contest

Run faster or you wont get your 5¢
Nike Maker 2,000
Just do it
Nike

Joel Patrie

Grade 8

Scotia-Glenville Junior High School

Scotia, New York

Third Place Winner Intermediate Level

1998 NewsCurrents Student Editorial Cartoon Contest

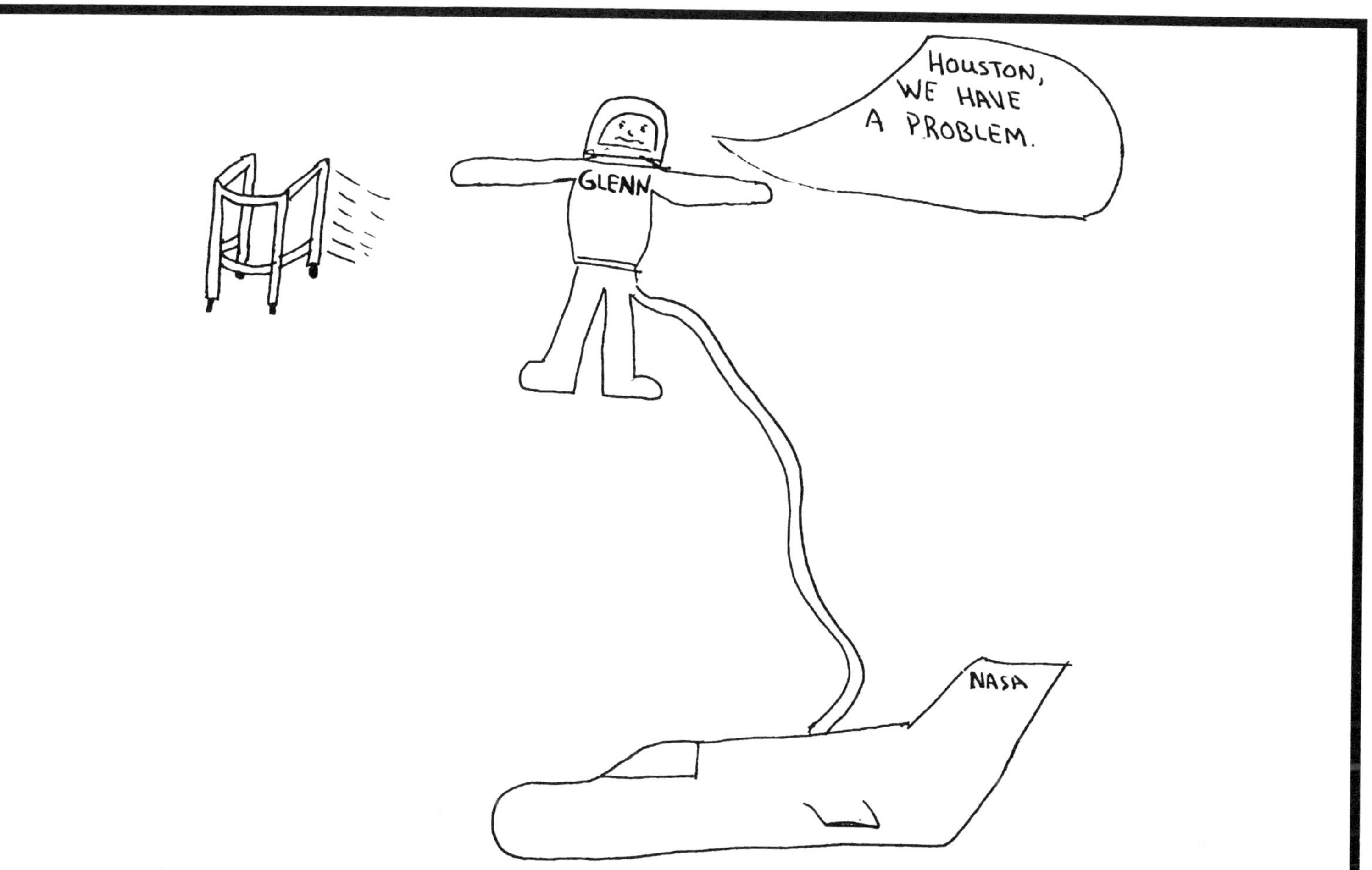
HOUSTON, WE HAVE A PROBLEM.
GLENN
NASA

Lauren van Houten and Heather Silverstein

Grade 8
Sherman Oaks C.E.S.
Reseda, California

Third Place Winner Intermediate Level
1998 NewsCurrents Student Editorial Cartoon Contest

NURSERY
HERE'S TO THE FUTURE!
MARLBORO
$ $ $
JOE
M

Anna Bertschy

Grade 7
Gravette Middle School
Gravette, Arkansas

The New Diet Plan!

Peter Johnson

Grade 7
Holy Family School
Orange, California

OK HIL,
SPRAY ME
GOOD. THAT OLD
COAT OF TEFLON
IS WEARING OFF!
Billy
TEF
By Peter Johnson 98

Seth Renz

Grade 7
Fall Creek Middle School
Fall Creek, Wisconsin

Feeding Frenzy

Jennifer Rock

Grade 7
Tamarac Middle School
Troy, New York

Iraq
Smallpox
Cholera
T.B.
E.coli
A Whole New Twist on Germination

Marian Andreescu

Grade 8
West Hills Middle School
West Bloomfield, Michigan

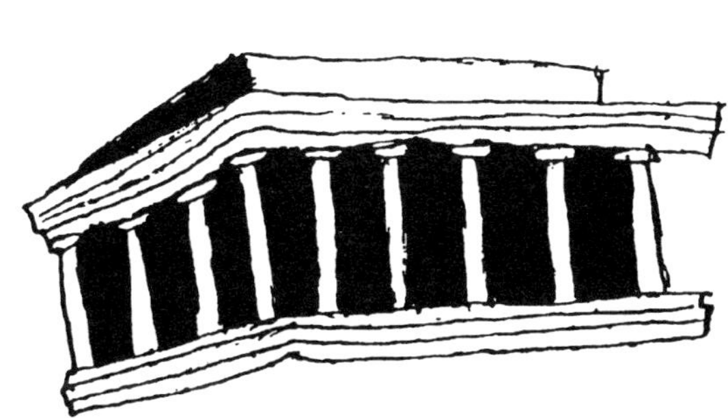

LINCOLN MEMORIAL

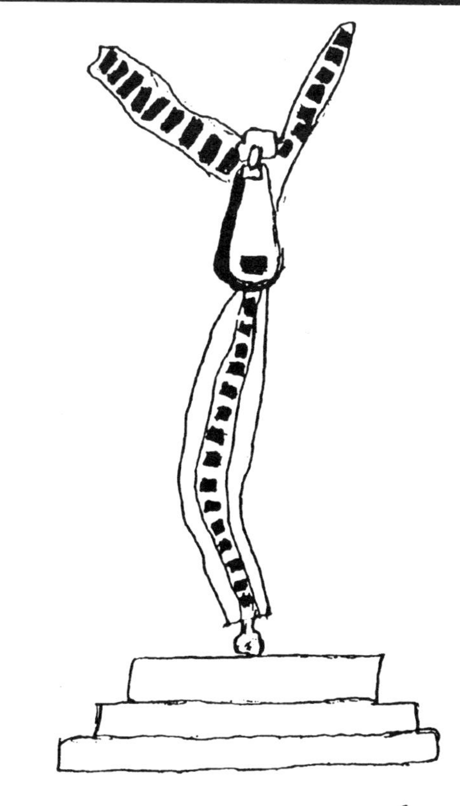

CLINTON MEMORIAL

Lyndsay Aspell

Grade 8
Our Lady of Good Counsel School
Moorestown, New Jersey

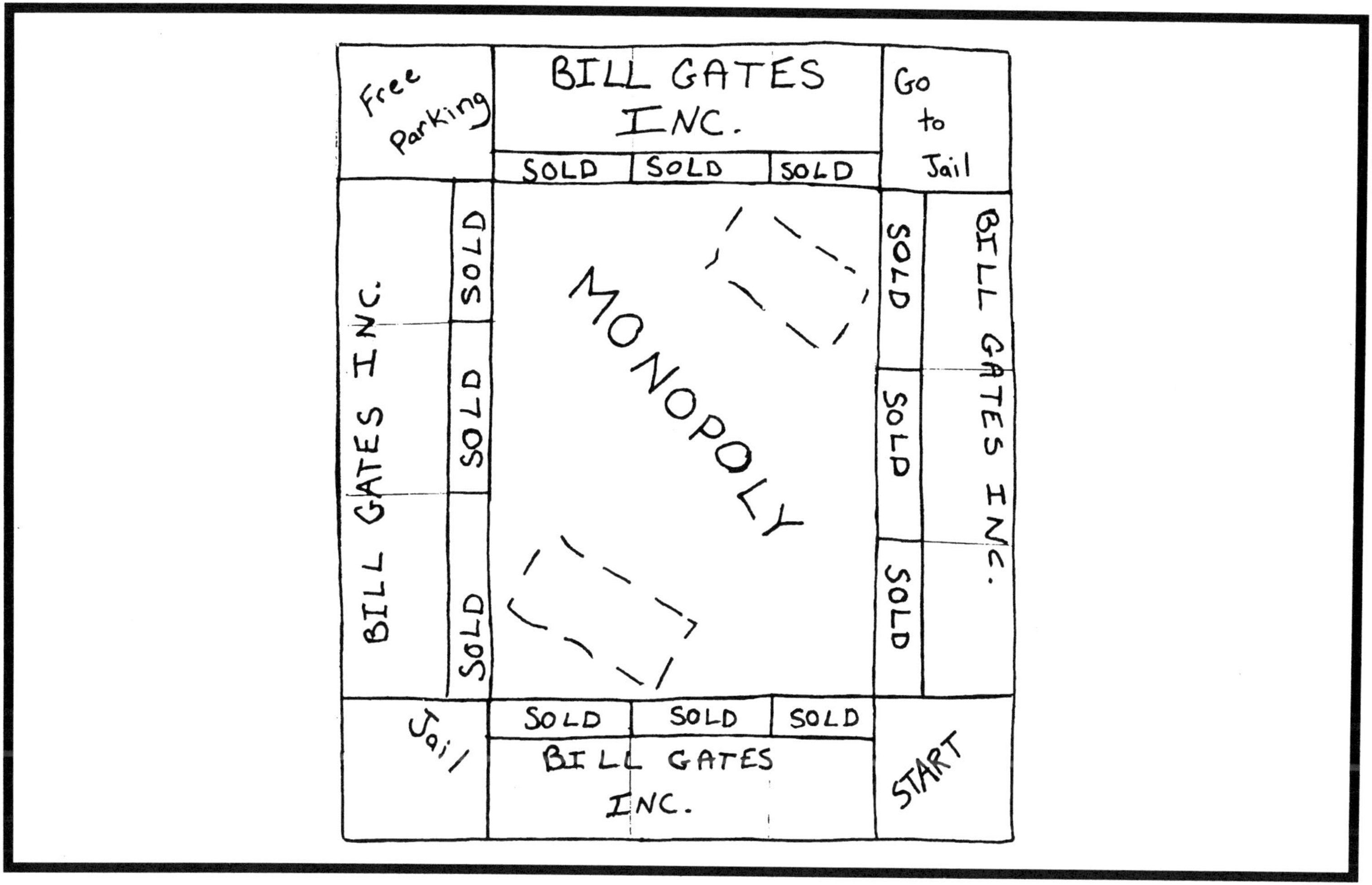

Free Parking

BILL GATES INC.

Go to Jail

SOLD SOLD SOLD

BILL GATES INC.

SOLD

SOLD

SOLD

MONOPOLY

SOLD

SOLD

SOLD

BILL GATES INC.

Jail

SOLD SOLD SOLD

BILL GATES INC.

START

Laura Broesamle

Grade 8
Kensington Academy
Beverly Hills, Michigan

without uniforms

with uniforms

Andrew Connell

Grade 8
Rogers Park Middle School
Danbury, Connecticut

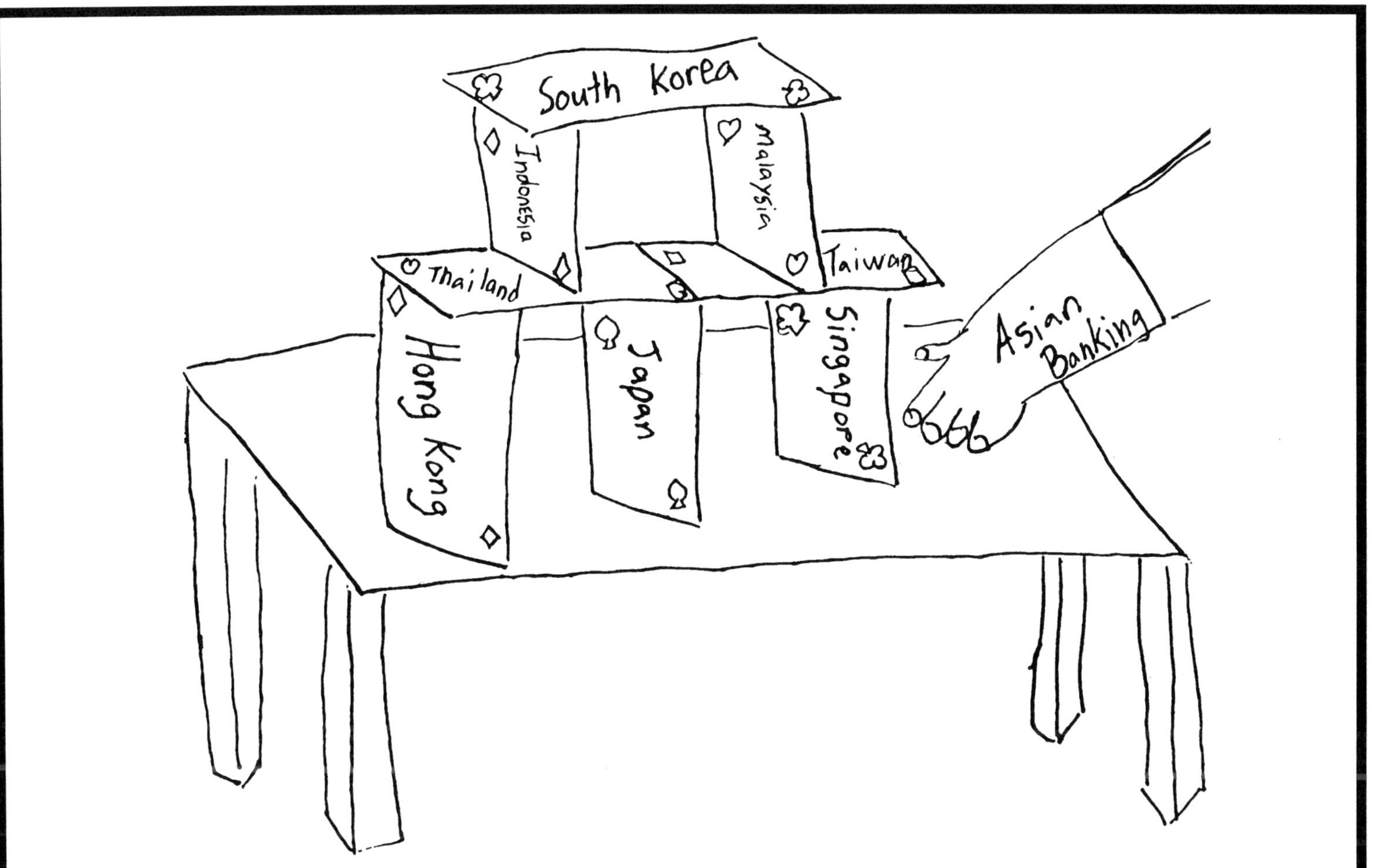
South Korea
Indonesia
Malaysia
Thailand
Taiwan
Hong Kong
Japan
Singapore
Asian Banking

Candace Dickow

Grade 8
West Hills Middle School
West Bloomfield, Michigan

CLINTON
REPUTATION

Jamie Eridon

Grade 8
Kensington Academy
Beverly Hills, Michigan

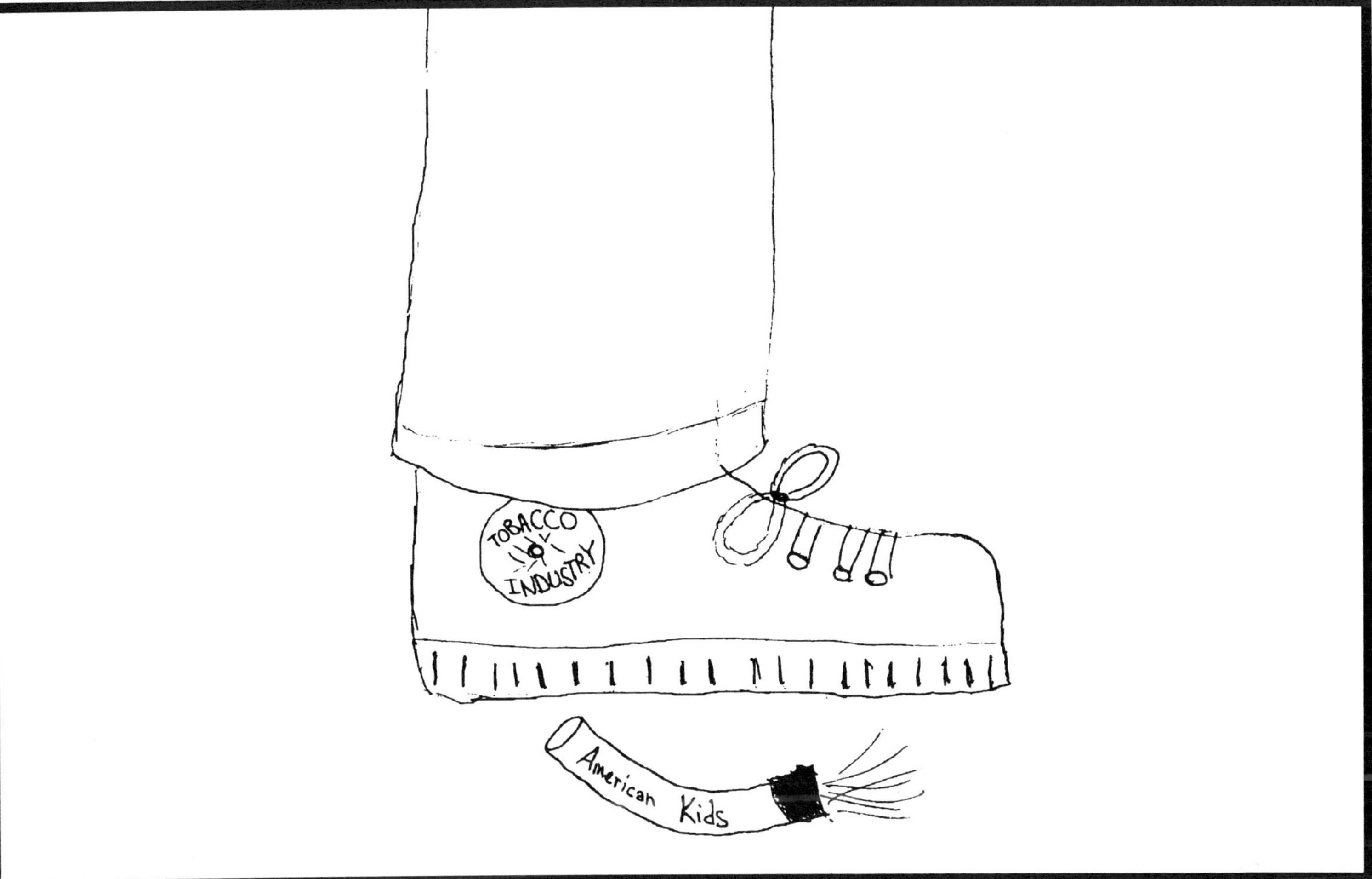
TOBACCO INDUSTRY
American Kids

Hilary Golston

Grade 8
Kensington Academy
Beverly Hills, Michigan

Gee, you would think we would get some of our money back.

tax payers

Deficit

Surplus

Social Security

Andrew Gowisnok

Grade 8
Wyoming Valley West Middle School
Kingston, Pennsylvania

STOCK MARKET
Daddy can we go on that ride?
No it's Too Scary.

Signe Hilton and Melissa Sachs

Grade 8
Sherman Oaks C.E.S.
Reseda, California

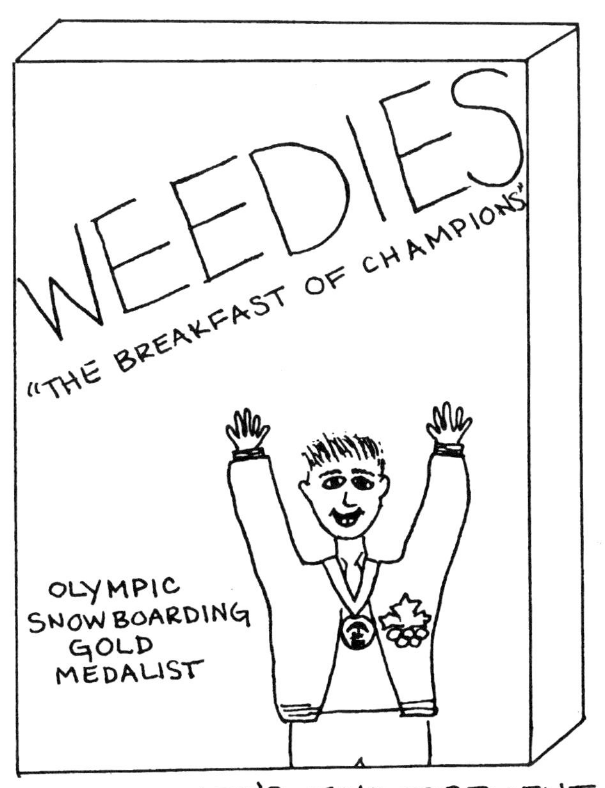

"ROSS REBAGLIATI'S ENDORSEMENT DEAL"

Signe-Hector,
Melissa Sachs

Tim Holden

Grade 8
Riverside Middle School
Watertown, Wisconsin

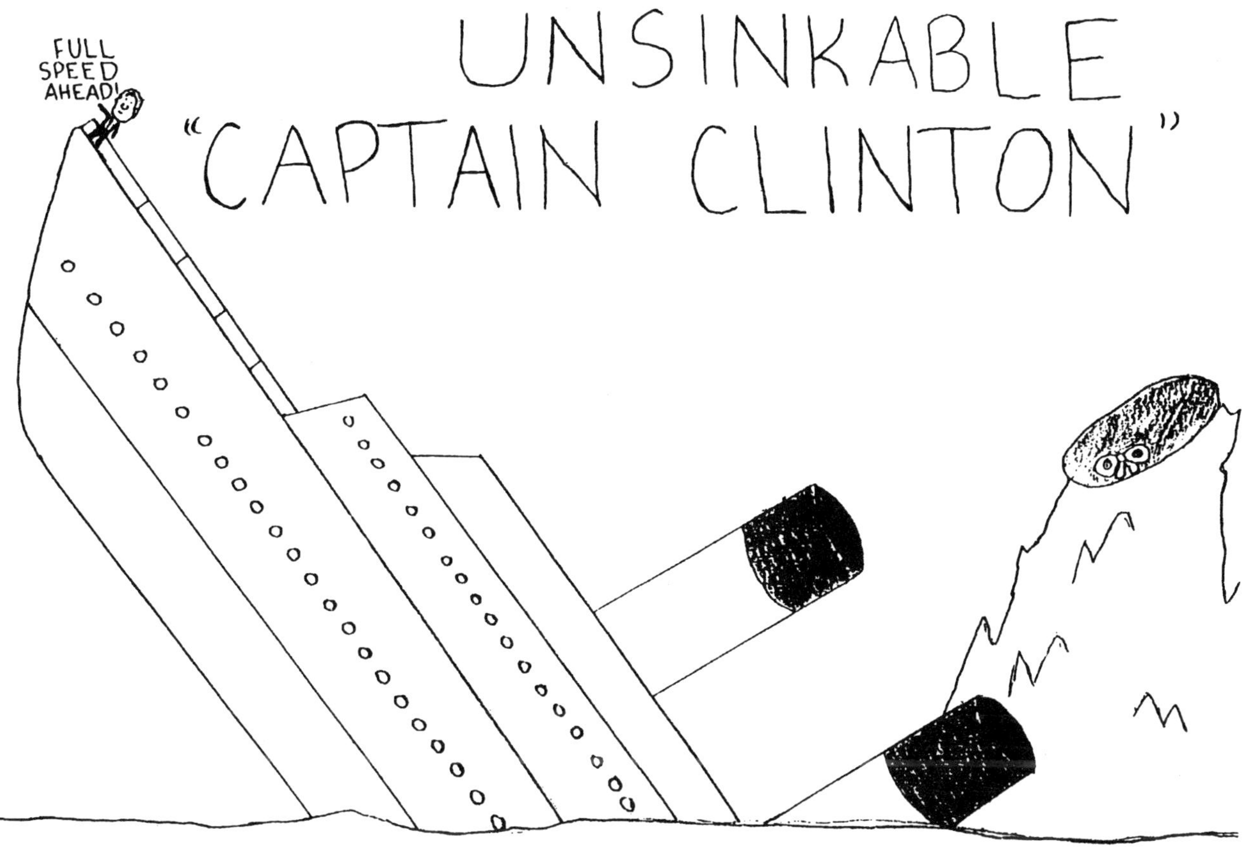
Tim Holden
UNSINKABLE
"CAPTAIN CLINTON"
FULL
SPEED
AHEAD!

Adam Isen

Grade 8
Sherman Oaks C.E.S.
Reseda, California

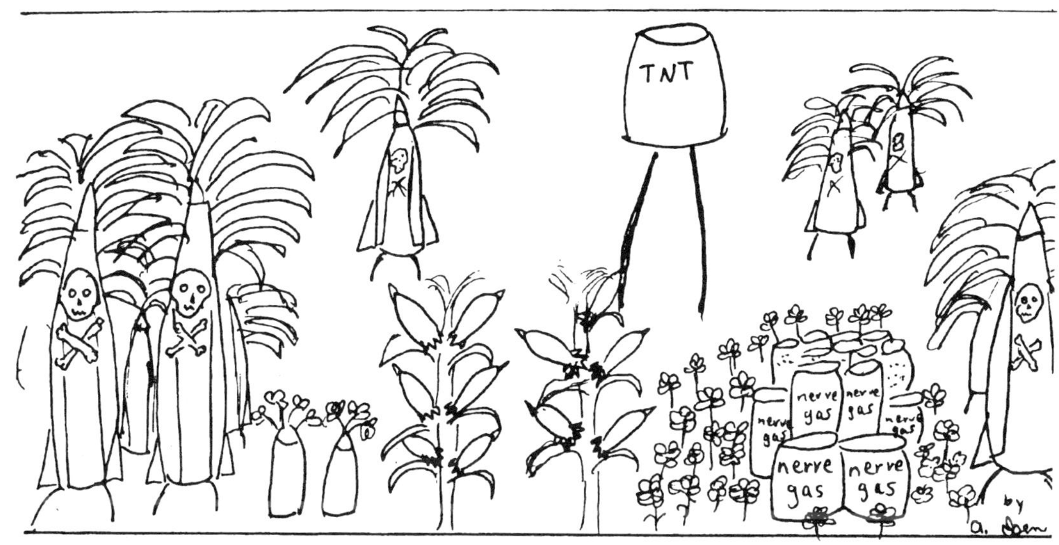

Saddam, Saddam, how does your garden grow?

Stephanie Karcutskie

Grade 8
Wyoming Area Secondary Center
Exeter, Pennsylvania

DR. KACZYNSKI'S CLASS
FINAL EXAMS Today!
YOUR FINAL EXAM GRADES WILL be MAILED to you!

David Knack

Grade 8
Living Word Academy
Syracuse, New York

What Communism
Got For
CHINA
U.S.
CHINA
TRADE
What Communism
Got For
CUBA
WARNING!
QUICKSAND
CUBA
U.S. EMBARGO
ON CUBA

Lindsey Levak

Grade 8
Amity Middle School
Amity, Oregon

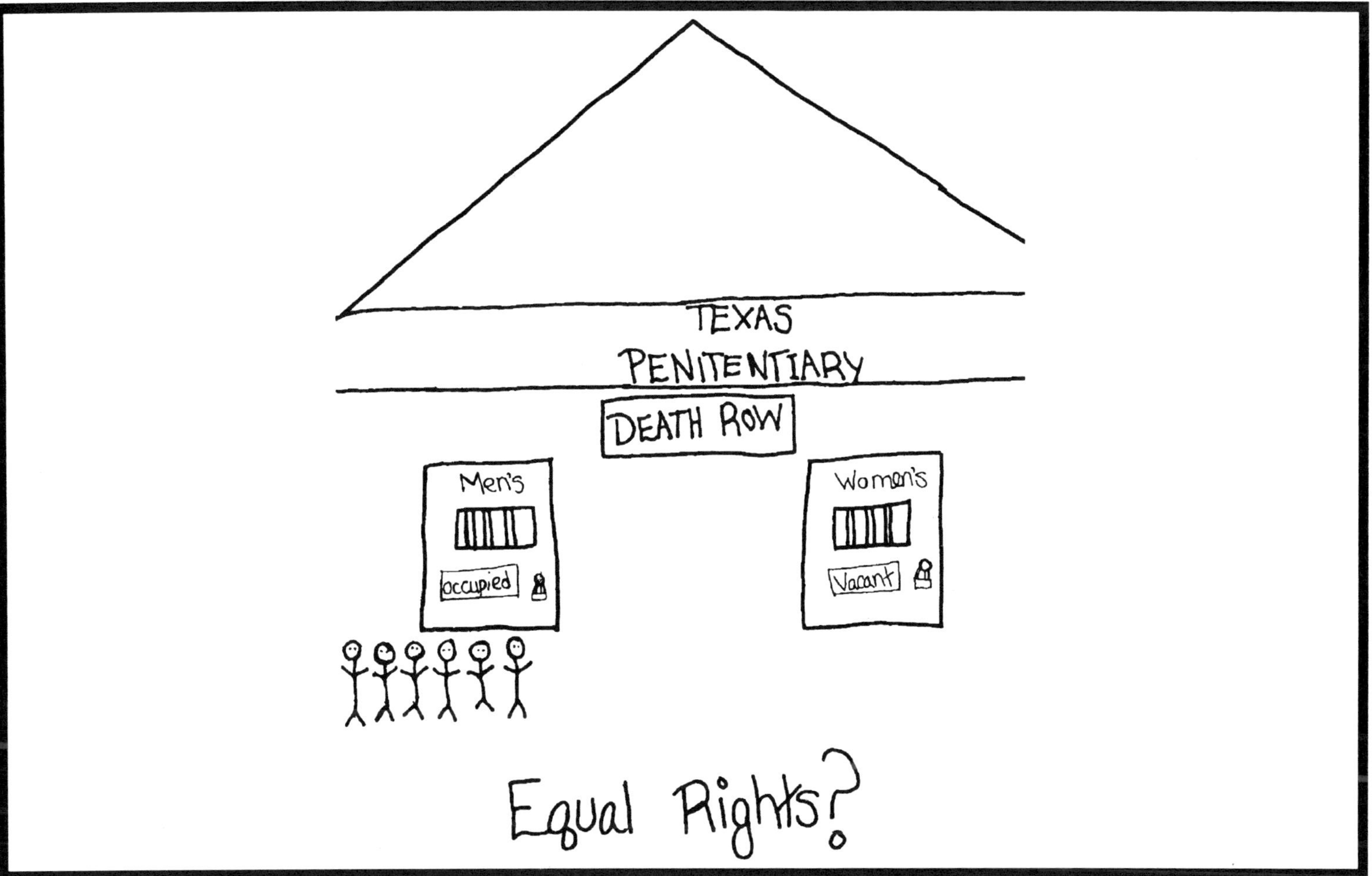
TEXAS
PENITENTIARY
DEATH ROW
Men's
occupied
Women's
Vacant
Equal Rights?

Sarah LoPatin

Grade 8
West Hills Middle School
West Bloomfield, Michigan

"Equal Opportunity?..."

Melissa Lutz

Grade 8
West Hills Middle School
West Bloomfield, Michigan

Keeping up with the Joneses.

Chris Magyar

Grade 8
Fall Creek Middle School
Fall Creek, Wisconsin

Stock Market
Slow
Asian Markets

Annie Mason

Grade 8
Amity Middle School
Amity, Oregon

Hey Man, What do ya think about that mad cow disease?
Well, I don't have to worry 'cause I'm a helicopter!
Mason 98'

Michael Montalbano

Grade 8
Spring-Ford Middle School
Royersford, Pennsylvania

NAGANO '98

James Powell

Grade 8
Chippewa Middle School
St. Paul, Minnesota

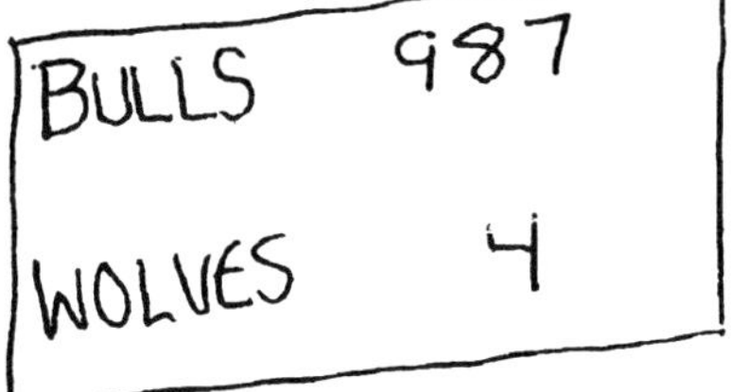
BULLS 987
WOLVES 4

Basketball, just hasn't been the same since the Jordan clonings.

Mike Scott

Grade 8
Kensington Academy
Beverly Hills, Michigan

U.S. ARMY
U.S.
Bosnia

William Seith

Grade 8
Rancho San Joaquin Middle School
Irvine, California

Why did the chicken cross the road?
BORDER
To get the HECK out of Hong Kong!
Come back here you sick chicken!... I kill you NOW!
Sickness is not a crime!

Brian Sharkey

Grade 8
St. Catherine of Siena
Wilmington, Delaware

He did it!
He did it!

Cloning Humans-
B-ah-ah-D
Dolly
Molly

Darryl Stein

Grade 8
Rancho San Joaquin Middle School
Irvine, California

IMF
Asian
Economy

Caroline Theoharides

Grade 8
Mattanawcook Junior High School
Lincoln, Maine

Jiang Zemin's New Look

Jordan Zlotoff

Grade 8
West Hills Middle School
West Bloomfield, Michigan

NASA
AARP
NASA
NASA

Joel DeBoef

Grade 9
Mona Shores High School
Muskegon, Michigan

From a look at the Nation's top computer, it is believed that we have been caught in a time warp
1900
In effect, starting tomorrow, Jan. 2, 1900, butter will go down to 2¢ per pound, and minimum wage will be at 17¢ per hour.

Brandon Deater

Grade 9
Mona Shores High School
Muskegon, Michigan

DR. KEVORKIAN'S
BATH TOY
To: Grandma
With Love

Jeanette Decker

Grade 9
Living Word Academy
Syracuse, New York

WHITE WATER
PAULA JONES
MONICA LEWINSKY
MORAL LEADER-SHIP
TRADE BALANCE
DOMESTIC POLICY
ASIAN CRISIS
MIDDLE EAST
FOREIGN POLICY

Tat Jung Lau

Grade 11
Bronx High School of Science
Bronx, New York

First Place Winner Senior Level
1998 NewsCurrents Student Editorial Cartoon Contest

TOMORROW? THEY'RE ALREADY PART OF TODAY'S BUSINESS.
COVER STORY
RJ REYNOLDS TOBACCO CAUGHT TARGETING 14 TO 24 YR. OLDS, WHO ARE "TOMORROW'S CIGARETTE BUSINESS."

Mellisa Cain

Grade 11
Scotia-Glenville High School
Scotia, New York

Second Place Winner Senior Level
1998 NewsCurrents Student Editorial Cartoon Contest

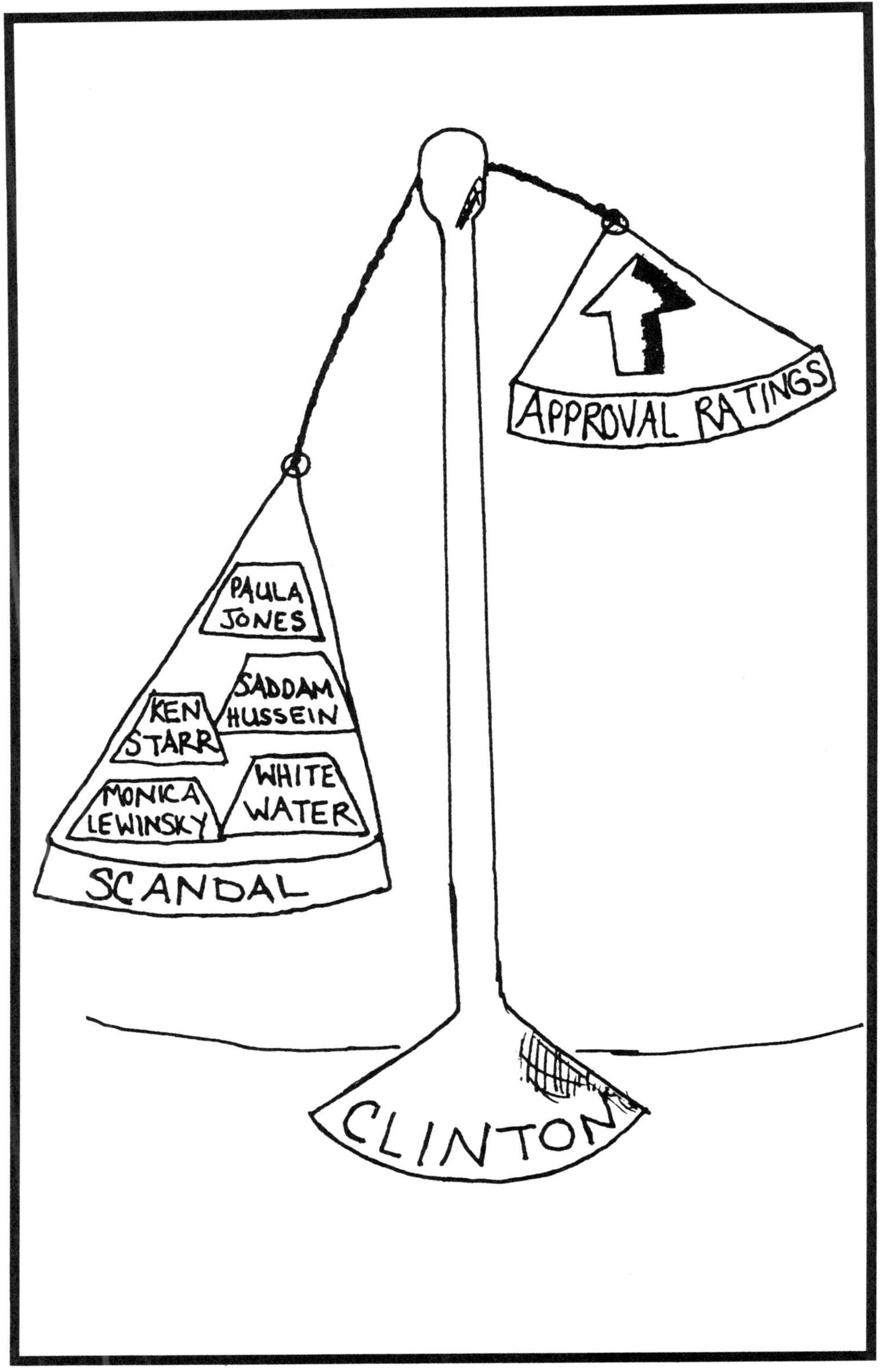
APPROVAL RATINGS
PAULA JONES
SADDAM HUSSEIN
KEN STARR
WHITE WATER
MONICA LEWINSKY
SCANDAL
CLINTON

Chris Engelbrecht

Grade 12
The Benjamin School
North Palm Beach, Florida

Second Place Winner Senior Level
1998 NewsCurrents Student Editorial Cartoon Contest

Brought to you by your friends at the Starr Company.

Tommie Sims

Grade 11
Muskegon High School
Muskegon, Michigan

Third Place Winner Senior Level
1998 NewsCurrents Student Editorial Cartoon Contest

WHAT COUID BE MORE DISGUSTING THAN A SAME-SEX MARRIAGE?
Congress
Special interest groups

Sarah Timm

Grade 11
Scotia-Glenville High School
Scotia, New York

Third Place Winner Senior Level
1998 NewsCurrents Student Editorial Cartoon Contest

Are you SURE this is a conspiracy?
BILL'S CLOSET

Lisa Vogtman

Grade 11
Towson Catholic High School
Towson, Maryland

Third Place Winner Senior Level
1998 NewsCurrents Student Editorial Cartoon Contest

TOURIST ATTRACTIONS OF THE 21ST CENTURY

BILL CLINTON SLEPT HERE...

AND HERE...

AND HERE...

AND HERE...

AND HERE...

AND HERE...

Justin Reed

Grade 11
Columbia High School
East Greenbush, New York

Third Place Winner Senior Level
1998 NewsCurrents Student Editorial Cartoon Contest

WHERE ARE YOU GETTING THESE HABITS, BOY!?
BAR
XXX
REED

Rob Backstrom

Grade 10
Muskegon High School
Muskegon, Michigan

BAR
of
Los Angeles
STOP
NO SMOKING
STOP!!
Read First
In this bar you can:
• Gamble
• Be Rude
• Make a fool of yourself
• And get drunk enough
to put yourself in a dangerous and possibly deadly situation, but
NO SMOKING!

Andrew Cheney

Grade 10
Yellow Springs High School
Yellow Springs, Ohio

Presidential POLLS
Before
After
SEX ED.
Although, sleeping around COULD help you, Shown Here
A. CHENEY

Andrea Daley

Grade 10
Heritage Academy
Hagerstown, Maryland

WAH!
WHA!
WAH!
WAH!
WHA!
WAH!
WAH!
BFI
7+
McCaughey's
SO MUCH FOR CRUCIAL WASTE-MANAGEMENT DECISIONS IN '98

Alma Mazer

Grade 10
Amherst Regional High School
Amherst, Massachusetts

NoNoNo!!! DON'T TOUCH THAT! YOU DON'T KNOW WHERE IT'S BEEN!
FOREIGN CONTRIBUTIONS
DONATIONS FROM UPPER-CLASS AMERICANS
CAMPAIGNING

Jeremy Potter

Grade 10
Heritage Academy
Hagerstown, Maryland

I better cover up this couch with this sheet.
SEXUAL HARASSMENT
CLINTON SEX SCANDAL
IRAQ

Mike Przybocki

Grade 10
Northern Cambria High School
Barnesboro, Pennsylvania

WANTED
NAGANO
FAILS
USA
SECOND
HAND?

Jeremy Savage

Grade 10
Heritage Academy
Hagerstown, Maryland

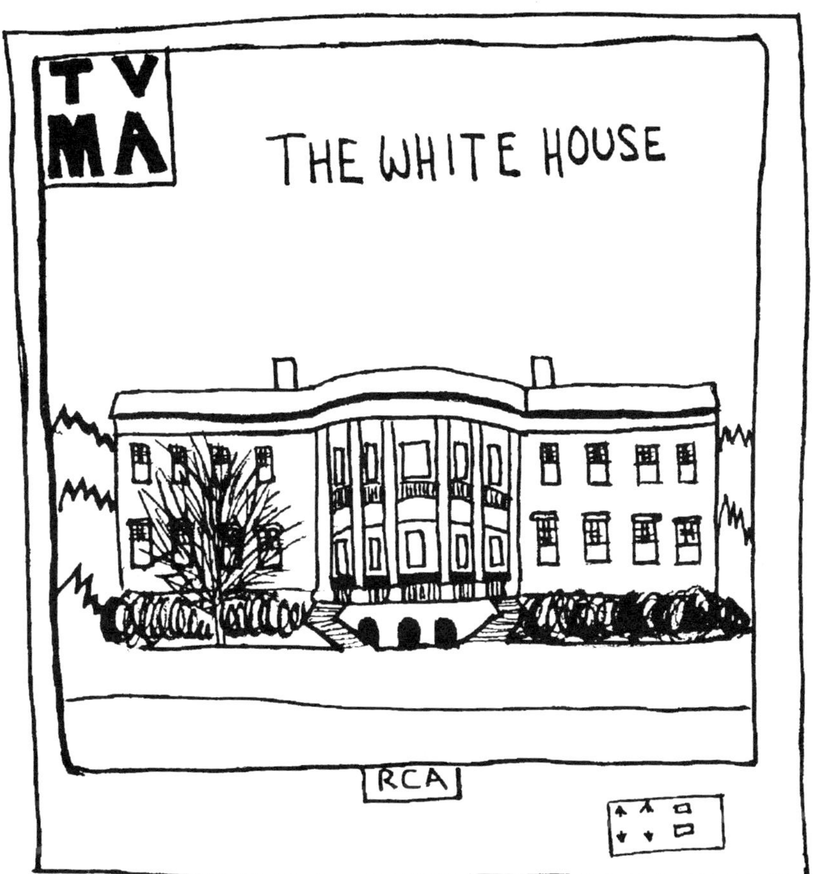

TV
MA
THE WHITE HOUSE
RCA

Joanna Temple

Grade 10
Heritage Academy
Hagerstown, Maryland

Health Care
Medicare
Welfare
Education
Social Security
Income
Clinton's Budget
Yes, we've finally managed to balance the budget!
POP!
RIP!
Baby Boomers .....

Devin Crockett

Grade 11
Muskegon High School
Muskegon, Michigan

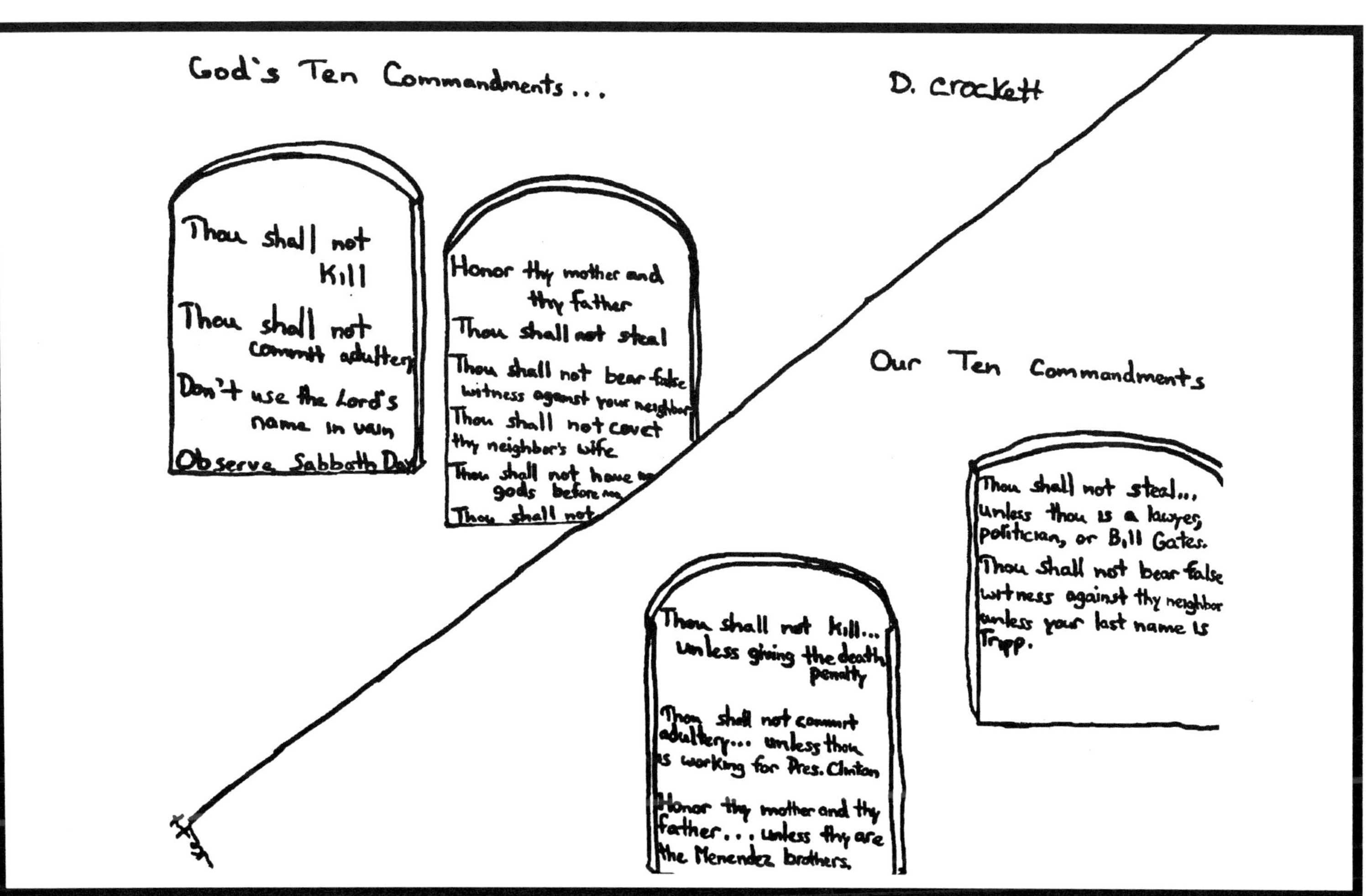
God's Ten Commandments...
D. Crockett
Thou shall not Kill
Thou shall not commit adultery
Don't use the Lord's name in vain
Observe Sabbath Day
Honor thy mother and thy father
Thou shall not steal
Thou shall not bear false witness against your neighbor
Thou shall not covet thy neighbor's wife
Thou shall not have no gods before me
Thou shall not
Our Ten Commandments
Thou shall not steal... unless thou is a lawyer, politician, or Bill Gates.
Thou shall not bear false witness against thy neighbor unless your last name is Tripp.
Thou shall not kill... unless giving the death penalty
Thou shall not commit adultery... unless thou is working for Pres. Clinton
Honor thy mother and thy father... unless thy are the Menendez brothers.

Travis Fisher

Grade 11
Elk County Christian High School
St. Marys, Pennsylvania

Social Security

President Clinton

Brett Hollis

Grade 11
Bob Jones High School
Madison, Alabama

The other athletes didn't care how the story went, they suspected steroids

Jonathan Hoogewind

Grade 11
Fruitport High School
Fruitport, Michigan

PRESIDENT CLINTON GETS ADVICE FROM TED KENNEDY

Sean Mathews

Grade 11
Poolesville High School
Poolesville, Maryland

NOW, IF IN THE FUTURE, WAR WITH IRAQ IS NECESSARY, I WANT YOU TO HANDLE IT THE WAY I WOULD HAVE
ENGLAND, HERE I COME
'98

Barry Rupprecht

Grade 11
Elk County Christian High School
St. Marys, Pennsylvania

USA'S MARK ON JAPAN

Lauren Fine

Grade 12
Highland Park High School
Dallas, Texas

FAGGOT!
BE LIKE CHRIST

Rafael Kushick

Grade 12
Amherst Regional High School
Amherst, Massachusetts

Foreign Policy
I'm telling you, it's there!
I Don't See any Dragon, Señor
USA

Valorie Ludovico

Grade 12
Living Word Academy
Syracuse, New York

WACC, TX
KENTUCKY
OKLAHOMA CITY
BILL CLINTON
IRAQ,
GET RID OF YOUR
WEAPONS OF MASS
DESTRUCTION!

Joe Scott

Grade 12
Muskegon Area Vocational Consortium
at Muskegon High School
Muskegon, Michigan

MEDIA
I DIDNT TOUCH HER- I SWEAR!
CLINTON ADMINISTRATION

Brett Smith

Grade 12
Muskegon High School
Muskegon, Michigan

Bill Gates Future Investments

Paula Stewart

Grade 12
Piedmont High School
Monroe, North Carolina

ROYAL FAMILY
MEDIA
PRINCESS DI
Paula Stewart '97

How to Enter the NewsCurrents Student Editorial Cartoon Contest

The NewsCurrents Student Editorial Cartoon contest is open to all elementary, middle, and high school students, including home scholars. Students may submit as many cartoons as they wish.

The cartoons submitted to the NewsCurrents Student Editorial Cartoon Contest must be the original ideas and work of the students who submit them. All submitted cartoons become the property of Knowledge Unlimited®, Inc., and may be used by Knowledge Unlimited and its divisions for promotional and other purposes at its discretion. Cartoons are judged primarily for originality, clarity of thought, and knowledge of the subject. Artistry is a secondary consideration, but it is certainly appreciated.

Some Suggestions

1. Study a number of professional cartoons to see what goes into them. Look at how cartoonists use symbols, caricature, exaggeration, and facial expression.
2. Select national news stories of major continuing interest — what's news in December may not be news in March, when the contest closes.
3. Don't clutter your cartoon with too many different ideas. The best editorial cartoons usually address one issue clearly.
4. Use black ink on white paper. Draw in bold lines. Keep lettering large enough to be read easily, even if it's reduced in size. Make sure that the lettering is legible.
5. Draw cartoons in a horizontal format rather than a vertical format.
6. Don't create a cartoon that is nothing more than a simple slogan ("Don't Smoke," "Save the Whales," etc.). Be thought-provoking and original. While your cartoon may express a widely held view of a leader or issue, it must be done in a fresh, original way.

For more information or contest rules, write to NewsCurrents Student Editorial Cartoon Contest — Contest Brochure, P.O. Box 52, Madison, WI 53701, or call (800)356-2303.